H.I.D.(HESS IS DEAD)

HOWARD BRENTON

Howard Brenton's many plays include *Christie in Love*, Portable
Theatre, 1969; *Revenge*, his first full-length stage play, Royal Court
Theatre Upstairs, 1969; *Hitler Dances*, Traverse Theatre Workshop,
Edinburgh, 1972; *Magnificence*, Royal Court Theatre, 1973;
Brassneck (written with David Hare), Nottingham Playhouse, 1973;
The Churchill Play, Nottingham Playhouse, 1974, and twice revived
by the Royal Shakespeare Company in 1978 and 1988; *Weapons of
Happiness*, National Theatre, 1976, winner of the Evening Standard
Best Play of the Year Award; *Epsom Downs*, Joint Stock Theatre
Company, 1977; *Sore Throats*, Royal Shakespeare Company, 1979;
The Romans in Britain, National Theatre, 1980; *Thirteenth Night*,
Royal Shakespeare Company, 1981; *The Genius*, Royal Court
Theatre, 1983; *Bloody Poetry*, Foco Novo, 1984, revived by the
Royal Court Theatre, 1988; *Pravda* (written with David Hare),
National Theatre, winner of the Evening Standard Best Play of the
Year Award, 1988; *Greenland*, Royal Court Theatre, 1988; and
Iranian Nights (written with Tariq Ali), Royal Court Theatre, and
televised on Channel Four by Bandung Productions, 1989. His
television plays include *A Saliva Milkshake*, BBC 1975; *The Paradise
Run*, Thames 1976; *Desert of Lies*, BBC 1984; and the four part
series *Dead Head*, BBC 1986. His first novel, *Diving for Pearls*, was
published in 1989 and he is presently writing another.

HOWARD BRENTON

H. I. D.

(HESS IS DEAD)

NICK HERN BOOKS

A division of Walker Books Limited

A Nick Hern Book

H.I.D. (Hess is Dead) first published in 1989 as an original paperback by Nick Hern Books, a division of Walker Books Limited, 87 Vauxhall Walk, London SE11 5HJ

H.I.D. (Hess is Dead) copyright © 1989 by Howard Brenton

Front cover picture by Mieke Visscher

Set in Baskerville by Book Ens, Saffron Walden, Essex
Printed by Billings & Sons, Worcester

British Library Cataloguing in Publication Data
Brenton, Howard, *1942-*
  Hess is dead.
  I. Title
  822'.914

ISBN 1-85459-046-4

Author's Note

H.I.D. (Hess is Dead) was conceived at the Mickery Theatre,
Amsterdam, in a series of exploratory and, for me,
explosively exciting discussions with the Mickery's Artistic
Director, Ritsaert ten Cate, in the Autumn of 1987 and the
Spring of 1988.

The Mickery's Dutch production is in preparation, under
the direction of Lodewijk de Boer, in a translation by de
Boer and Anthony Akerman and opens, *pace* the disasters
to which all artistic endeavours are prone, in Amsterdam
on 7 December 1989, not in a theatre but in the Waag.

The Waag is an old customs house that once stood at
one of the gates of the city. At its centre there is a
seventeenth-century dissecting room, a place of
enlightenment and science. Criminals hanged just outside
the gate were rushed, fresh, to the dissecting room, where
their humanity was laid bare by the surgeon's knife to
medical students and any interested citizens, who paid for
admittance. On the domed ceiling the famous doctors, who
cut the dead beneath to enlighten the public, had their
names and badges of office painted above a lengthy Latin
inscription which, more or less, reads, 'The lives of the
dead examined here were worthless, but in death they aid
our understanding of life.' The resonances of performing
this play, which attempts to dissect the murky entrails of
the 'truth' of Rudolf Hess's death in Spandau prison using
the unscientific precision of drama, in this famous room,
are far-reaching. To present such a play there of all places
is a typical piece of Mickery cultural mischief-making.

Meanwhile the Mickery, who commissioned the play and
own the performance rights, have with great generosity
licensed the Royal Shakespeare Company to present the
play at the Almeida Theatre. The two productions are
entirely separate in conception and in their casts (the
author is in the exciting, though somewhat bizarre
predicament of going from one powerfully imaginative
director in London, to another in Amsterdam. Jokes about
the Dutch production, which will start rehearsing after the

RSC opens the play, are flying about the British rehearsal room . . . e.g. 'Of course when the Dutch do this scene naked and underwater . . .').

I am very grateful to both theatres who have linked hands across a considerable gulf of different theatre practices, almost different worlds, to make the English production possible.

Anyone writing about the death of Hess has to be indebted to *Hess: A Tale of Two Murders* by Hugh Thomas (Hodder & Stoughton), which is not at all the 'lunatic fringe' book which the British Government wishes it were. I also want to thank Richard Norton-Taylor, who has pursued the story of the 'Hess Affair' relentlessly in *The Guardian*, and who very kindly sent me a file of remarkable material. Needless to say, they are not responsible for any of the speculations in the play.

Howard Brenton

H. I. D.

(HESS IS DEAD)

'As for the present, leaving history aside for the moment, I warn you I shall complain to the management.'

Mikhail Bulgakov
The Master and Margarita

Characters

PALMER
CHARITY
NICOLE
OFFICER
RAYMOND
LUBER (*unseen*)

H.I.D. (*Hess is Dead*) was first staged at the Almeida Theatre, London, by the Royal Shakespeare Company. First preview was 26 September 1989; press night was 28 September 1989.

The cast was as follows:

LARRY	David Calder
CHARITY	Polly Walker
NICOLE	Diane Fletcher
RAYMOND	Pip Donaghy
OFFICER	Mark Strong
LUBER (unseen)	

Directed by Danny Boyle

Designed by Eryl Ellis & Kenny McLellan
Lighting by Geraint Pugh
Video by Ian Francis
Stage manager Jane Pole
Deputy stage manager Sheonagh Darby
Assistant stage managers Kate Sarley & Paul Fooks

Hess is Dead was a Mickery Theatre project by Howard Brenton and Ritsaert ten Cate

A room of tapestries which hang from a great height, but which do not quite reach the ground. The tapestries form a quadrangular room. The tapestries are blue. They have a trompe l'oeil *effect, describing a room in a late seventeenth century palace. With the movement of performers, members of the audience, or draughts, the tapestries swing. They should be heavy, or, if of paper, weighted, so that their movement is languid. About the 'room' there are gold, upright chairs, for the audience to sit upon and for the performers to use. If, because of fire regulations, the audience's chairs have to be bound together, they should be bound in clumps. The audience would then 'sit about' the room, in irregular groups. Between the chairs are television monitors on trolleys, which the audience can move for their own convenience. A central VTR machine, upon which the performers sometimes play video tapes, is also on a mobile trolley. There should be a sense that the whole space is 'bugged', tense with multip' recording devices, audio and visual.*

I.

LARRY PALMER, *sitting upon a chair. He is waiting. By the chair, a large briefcase.*

Watch and wait. He watches his hands, waiting.

PALMER.   You say

         yes, that's

               what I

   Believe in, that's

        my certainty

             in the back

   Of my head.

       No, neck

           spine

   Lodged between

> the shoulder blades
>> my moral self

What I
> believe, a lump
>> just beneath

The skin. Part
> of me, taken
>> for granted

A bit of bone
> a bit of gristle
>> a vertebra

A sense
> of right
>> and wrong

Part of you
> inert, just
>> lodged there

Year in, year out
> not giving
>> the slightest ache.

A silence. PALMER *still.*

Then he straightens his back. Moves a shoulder uncomfortably.

He shrugs and slumps, staring down at his shoe.

A silence, he is still.

Then he leans forward and picks at a piece of dirt, stuck to the toe cap. He stops.

> Then one day
>> you are challenged.
>>> It doesn't need

The point of a knife
> the muzzle
>> of a gun

Just a simple
> killer
>> question

A sudden
     killer
          look

Into your
     face – 'Right
          you bastard

What
     do
          YOU

Stand for?'
     And you are
          struck dumb

You panic
     your neck
          locks solid

You can't
     turn
          your head

Your spine
     is glass, rigid
          fragile, it

Could splinter
     cripple you
          there and then.

'I . . .
     believe, I . . .'
          but what?

He pauses. A little laugh to himself, smiling.

His smile fades.

You cannot say
     for you have always
          at parties

At work
     on the 'phone
          assumed that you

Were 'in the right'

that of course
you 'stood for the good'

But never really
said what
good, what

Right and at the moment
of maximum danger
the knife

Point, the
terrible look
you realise

'I stand
for nothing
at all

I have never had to
in my life
in the West

In the long, long peace
on the long, long march
of democracy

To the McDonald's
hamburger restaurant
chain, I

Need no
belief
at all

I believe
nothing
at all.'

A silence. Then he shrugs.

Freedom
is
fast food.

That is my position and it suits
me very well, I am a journalist
let others stand, believe and bleed

            For great
                        causes, I
                                    just want

            A
                        good
                                    story.

    CHARITY LUBER *comes on.* PALMER *stands.*

CHARITY. Mr Palmer?

    They shake hands.

PALMER. Vielen Dank, dass Sie mich empfangen, Frau
Luber, ich hoffe es geht Ihnen gut.

    She waves a hand.

    A pause.

    *They sit, facing each other, but with an odd distance between
them, a little too far from each other for comfort.*

Ich bin Ihnen wirklich sehr dankbar fur dieses
Interview.

CHARITY. Please, we'll speak English.

PALMER. A relief, thank you. I am a typical Englishman,
locked in my own language.

    He smiles, she does not.

Frau Luber, I'd like to say . . . how distressed I was to
hear of your husband's death. He was the most
brilliant man. Please do accept my condolences.

    A silence.

CHARITY. Did you know Istvan?

PALMER. I did, luckily, interview him once. For the
Atlantic Review.

CHARITY. Was he rude to you?

PALMER. Not at all.

CHARITY. Then you must have bored him.

PALMER. I was aware of his legendary . . . difficulty? But I found him a delight. He gave me some excellent material.

CHARITY. Oh Istvan always gave excellent material. I was a student of his in Geneva. We married. I was young.

PALMER. Yes.

A silence.

Frau Luber, do you want to see the questions I have prepared for this interview, before I ask them?

CHARITY. No, ask what you want. Do you mind if I smoke?

PALMER. . . . Should you?

CHARITY. Zoot. This sanitorium costs a fortune. At these prices, the patients can do anything, even die.

She removes two ashtrays from a handbag. They are small, of clear cut-glass.

I carry ashtrays, for myself and my guests.

PALMER. How do you know I smoke?

CHARITY. Your teeth are stained.

PALMER. Ah.

She holds out one of the ashtrays. He stands, leaning forward to take it. She does not release it.

CHARITY. Do you assume, because I'm in this place, that I'm sick?

PALMER. I . . .

CHARITY. Sick in my head? 'Out of my tree?'

PALMER. I . . . have no idea, Frau Luber.

CHARITY. There is a room here, where they hose you down, naked. With high pressure jets.

PALMER *is stuck in his position, the ashtray held between them.*

PALMER. I thought this was the . . . most advanced sanitorium in Europe?

CHARITY. Oh it is.

> *She lets go of the ashtray.* PALMER *returns to his seat. He
> sets the ashtray on the floor beside his foot. He lights a cigarette.*
> CHARITY *watches him as he exhales and crosses his legs. As
> if this were a signal, she in turn takes out a cigarette and lights
> it. Then she continues.*

The most expensive psychotherapy has abandoned
psychoanalysis. All that talk? It's out. Now you pay a
fortune for a hard cold shower. It doesn't work, of
course. But did Freud, Adler, Jung?

PALMER. I . . .

> *A shrug at the enormity of the subject.*

. . . have a crude soul, Frau Luber. I have avoided the
psychiatrist's couch.

CHARITY. Yes. The crude amongst us always shine with
health.

> *She watches for the insult's effect. He smiles.*

Please, set up your tape-recorder. I assume you have
no shorthand?

PALMER. Forgive me, no.

CHARITY. Few journalists under fifty do.

PALMER. Do you object?

CHARITY. Istvan said that the written word tells less lies
than the taped.

PALMER. I can send you a full transcript of our
conversation, for your comments . . .

CHARITY. No.

> PALMER *caught, looking at her.*

PALMER (*aside*). Playing the Grande Dame.

CHARITY (*aside*). A journalist. Why do Englishmen always
seem so . . . damp?

PALMER (*aside*). Tight bum, good tits. German?

CHARITY (*aside*). A wet Englishman, from his ditchwater island.

PALMER (*aside*). Or Swiss? Hard boiled. And young.

CHARITY (*aside*). But I must make him understand, I have no choice.

PALMER (*aside*). The new European woman. Skin cream and enemas, theories of the health of the liver, a skier's calf muscles, all very EEC. Am I intimidated? Yes, I am intimidated.

PALMER *still caught looking at* CHARITY, *who speaks aside.*

CHARITY. I married
                        an old
                                    man, with

                Profound relief
                        I left the youthful zoo
                                    of peacock feathers

                Motorbikes, hanging about
                        inadequately hung
                                    young men

She laughs.

                                    I
                Cut out from
                        my generation
                                    to go nun-like

                To an old
                        man's bed
                                    an old man's

                Dreams, in my arms
                        and in my dreams
                                    all his ghosts

                His dead friends
                        long gone lovers
                                    clutched to me

                With Istvan I made love
                        to lost hope

lost happiness

The caresses
of the grateful
dead.

She laughs, throwing her head back.

Oh the

Desperate
desperate
nights

For the old man
was not defeated
he raged

And a sexist pig
no gratitude
from him

That he'd got his hands
on young flesh, oh no!
No shyness

No shame at the softness
in parts about
his belly

The reversion to babyhood
that old men
endure –

See him play tennis
thwunk! the games –
player, shoulders

Heaved, rounded
in long blue shorts
naked to pot –

Bellied waist
snarling, thwunk!
at the net

An opponent
wrong-footed
smashed. Rage –

In everything
        that rage
                in love

Rage. Now, I
        the widow
                carry

The burning
        the crucible
                of his molten

Fury
        condemned
                to burn

And talk of a dead husband
        to wet young men –
                into tape-recorders.

PALMER. So I may . . . ?

She waves her cigarette. He takes out a tape-recorder from his briefcase. He stands. He pulls a chair between them, puts the recorder upon it. He returns to his chair. With a remote control, he starts the tape.

Nothing for a moment. Then the tape is heard. An American woman's voice, rich and calm.

TAPE. This statement is issued on the 17th of September, 1987 by the four powers, the Union of Soviet Socialist Republics, the United States of America, the United Kingdom and France.

PALMER *stops the tape. He speaks quickly.*

PALMER. This is the statement put out by the four powers in Berlin after Rudolf Hess's death. This tape was prepared by the Americans for their news agencies. I got this copy off a mate on Voice of America. It's ace. (*He restarts the tape.*)

TAPE. One. The four powers are now in a position to make a final statement on the death of Rudolf Hess.

A pause.

Two. Investigations have confirmed that on the 17th of

August Rudolf Hess hanged himself from a window latch in a small summer house in the prison garden, using an electrical extension cord which had for some time been kept in the summer house for use in connection with a reading lamp. Attempts were made to revive him and he was then rushed to the British Medical Hospital where, after further unsuccessful attempts to revive him, he was pronounced dead at 16.10 hours.

A pause.

Three. A note addressed to Hess's family was found in his pocket. This note was written on the reverse side of a letter from his daughter-in-law dated 20th July, 1987. It began with the words: 'Please would the Governors send this home. Written a few minutes before my death.' The senior document examiner from the laboratory of the British Government Chemist, Mr P.A.M. Beard, has examined the note, and concluded that he can see no reason to doubt that it was written by Rudolf Hess.

A pause.

Four. A full autopsy was performed on Hess's body on the 19th of August in the British Military Hospital by Dr J. Malcolm Cameron. The autopsy was conducted in the presence of medical representatives of the Four Powers. The report noted a linear mark on the left side of the neck consistent with a ligature. Dr Cameron stated that in his opinion death resulted from asphyxia, caused by the compression of the neck due to suspension.

The tape runs on for a while. A silence. Then PALMER *stops it.*

PALMER. That is what I reported at the time. The official line.

CHARITY. The official truth.

PALMER. Indeed.

CHARITY. Which you now no longer believe?

A silence.

PALMER. May I? The tape . . .

She waves her hand, looking away. PALMER *starts the tape.*

Frau Luber, why did your husband predict that Hess would be murdered in Spandau?

CHARITY. Istvan predicted many things. His enemies accused him of being a poet, posing as a critic. As to the reality of what he predicted . . .

A wave of the cigarette in her hand.

PALMER. I am aware of the attacks made upon your husband. I have always been suspicious of them, because he was Jewish.

Nothing from CHARITY. *Now* PALMER *is careful with his next sentence.*

And he died at the same time as Hess, the very same day as the man whose reality he pursued so relentlessly.

CHARITY. The poetry of coincidence, Mr Palmer.

PALMER. A difficult concept, Frau Luber.

CHARITY. I'd rather believe in coincidence, rather than in fate, wouldn't you?

PALMER. I don't know. I . . . have a rather prosaic nature.

CHARITY. Yes?

PALMER. It's an English trait.

CHARITY. Nevertheless you've become an obsessive.

PALMER. I'm sorry?

CHARITY. A 'Hess freak'.

PALMER. Oh I think not.

She smiles.

CHARITY. No?

PALMER. I'm just here for a good story, to sell, Frau Luber. I am just a rat-faced journalist, poking my nose

into things, into your life, actually, Frau Luber.
Twitching my whiskers.

Still, she smiles. He is unnerved.

But. But . . .

PALMER *sighs. He leans forward, his elbows upon his knees.*

In my trade, facts are all. They are stones. Stones are
real. That was said, that was done. But hard facts can,
I find, go . . . mushy. The stones turn to
marshmallow. The . . . assassination of John Kennedy?
Was there a second gunman? The death of Mozart,
poisoned by Salieri? The world has seen *Amadeus*, the
movie. Actually, Salieri was a good friend to Mozart.
Who was not a pauper, but a man with a carriage and
servants. Not poisoned, he just caught the 'flu. But
once the world has seen the movie . . . And the true
horror of the Nazi death camps, which cannot be
shown on American TV because of the sponsors?
Dachau and Sobibor have to be cleaned up for the
viewers and, by American TV mini-series, the true
horror dies. Hard facts become 'beliefs'. Puffs of
smoke. Phantoms. Stones to burnt marshmallow.

A silence.

CHARITY. Istvan said that, by 1970, Germany had won
the Second World War.

She eyes him.

True or false?

PALMER. Frau Luber, your husband was a relentless
champion of historical truth.

CHARITY *is exasperated.*

CHARITY. A champion of . . . Mr Palmer!

She regains her temper.

If you asked most people under thirty, 'Who was
Rudolf Hess?', how many would say 'He was Hitler's
deputy?' How many would know that he was the ghost
writer for Hitler's *Mein Kampf*? How many would know
what *Mein Kampf* was? How many would know that

Hess flew a Messerschmidt 110, on a mad solo flight, from Germany to Scotland, on the 10th of May, 1941? I'm not talking about students of history, just people, under thirty, around the streets, in London, Paris, Amsterdam, in Berlin. I mean who cares? The death of Rudolf Hess?

A flick of the hand.

It was something on TV. Zoot.

PALMER. You care.

CHARITY. I am condemned to. I could . . . Walk out of this place. Get on a motorbike now, with a man my age, go to the south. The mountains of Provence, the Luberon. I could be making love under the stars in the south, 48 hours from now.

She stands, suddenly. She approaches the video trolley.

This is a tape my husband made.

She laughs.

Istvan loved fooling about with cameras. He was like you, Mr Palmer.

PALMER. How do you mean?

CHARITY. 'Nosey.' A voyeur, a peeping Tom.

PALMER. I didn't . . .

CHARITY. He would even video us making love. But he was always messing up the cameras. Video was just graffiti to him. This tape's typical.

She touches buttons. The lights change. The monitors fuzz into life.

II.

There are three elements in this sequence.

A: A video tape made, presumably by ISTVAN LUBER, *of* CHARITY *miming Rudolf Hess's physical state and his death. It is in black and white. It has been made in what seems to be a chaotic hotel room, suitcases with their contents pulled out, an unmade bed. The video is shown on the monitors throughout the playing area and the audience.*

B: CHARITY's *live commentary on the video and* PALMER's *reactions to it. She repeats the mimed gestures she makes upon the tape.*

C: A dance which, step by step, in fragments, she builds as she describes HESS *and his death. These dance fragments are very brief and sudden. (The idea of the dance is that from the pitiful, sordid state of* HESS's *old age that she mimes, she is choreographing something that is, unacceptably, beautiful – the dance.)*

1. Tape.

Black and white photographs of Rudolf Hess. A kaleidoscope. Irregular cutting, each held for different lengths of time. ('Graffiti'.) His days with Hitler. Uniformed. Then as a pilot. At Nuremberg in the dock, the photograph of Goering laughing at him. The exterior of Spandau. The photograph of Hess dead in the mortuary.

2. Live.

CHARITY. The sound's all screwed up. And you'll know these Hess pix.

PALMER. The same old pix. When was this made?

CHARITY. Istvan put it together, now and then.

PALMER. Do you think the pictures of Hitler and Co. will ever wear out?

CHARITY. Istvan was afraid they'd change. Slowly. That even the negatives, in the archives, would become lies.

A pause, the montage on the tapes continuing.

What he was really afraid of was that they would become beautiful.

PALMER. What do you mean? What . . . did Istvan mean?

CHARITY *(casually)*. Oh, that the death camps would become art.

A pause.

That, in the next century, there will be adverts for Hamburgers, set in Belsen?

PALMER. No.

CHARITY. No what?

PALMER. Just no. Memory could never decay that much . . .

CHARITY. One of Istvan's themes was that all history decays.

PALMER. But not Belsen.

CHARITY. Why not? Isn't the Emperor Nero just a joke now? Isn't Napoleon used to sell brandy?

Wait, until the image of Hess dead in the mortuary.

PALMER. Stop.

CHARITY. What?

PALMER. Stop the tape.

She does so, at the image of Hess, dead.

That's Hess in the mortuary. How did Luber get that on to the tape? He died the day Hess died.

CHARITY. I put it there.

A pause.

PALMER. Ah.

CHARITY. This montage went on for three cassettes, I cut it down.

PALMER. When? I mean, in here?

CHARITY. Oh yes. There's a full video-editing suite in the sanitorium's basement. My psychiatrists see it as part of my therapy. I paid for it. I am a very rich woman, Mr Palmer, I inherited everything Istvan had. If I am to go insane, I don't see why I shouldn't do it with state-of-the-art equipment.

PALMER. No. No.

CHARITY. This next sequence is as Istvan left it.

She runs the tape.

3. Tape.

The tape continues. The wrecked bedroom. **CHARITY** *stands dead still, seen full-length, a neutral position, arms loose at her sides. She is barefoot. She wears a light-coloured ballet dancer's leotard.*

4. Live.

CHARITY. Rudolf Hess in August 1987.
    Age, ninety-three.
    Imprisoned since 1947.
    Much of his physical strength gone. Capable of little effort.
    Suffered a minor stroke in the late seventies.
    Circulatory problems in the brain.
    Both eyes affected, nearly blind in the right.

5. Tape.

Her hand goes to her left eye.

(NB: from here her live commentary follows her twisting distortions on the tape, as, detail by detail, her young dancer's body assumes the

physical state of the old man. She repeats them live, breaking into the
dancing steps where indicated.)

6. Live.

> *Following the tape.*

CHARITY. Left arm.
   Elbow bent.
   Shoulder frozen.
   No grip in the hand, great pain.
   Movement restricted.
   To the front, arm cannot be raised above the
   horizontal.
   And to the side, no more than 45 degrees.

7. Dance.

Suddenly, using the mimed gestures, a dancing movement with her
left arm, of a twisted grace.

8. Tape.

She stops the mime and, no sound, she· is talking to someone off
camera about what to do next. She appears to be angry. She gestures
and stamps her foot, turning away from the camera, then back to it.

9. Live.

PALMER. Is that Istvan, talking to you?

CHARITY. He should have gone to Hollywood, with all
   the others.

PALMER. Forgive me, but Hollywood this is not.

CHARITY. I meant gone with all the other exiles to
   America, in 1933.

PALMER. Ah.

Whatever the discussion on the tape was, it is resolved.
CHARITY *continues, following her mime on the tape.*

CHARITY. Right arm.
Can raise the hand to comb his hair, feebly. Needs a
big comb to do so.
His coffee mug.
Since 1979, too heavy to hold by the handle.
Writing.
Cannot with the right hand more than a few minutes.
Cramps, stiffness.
Walking.
Balance bad, affected by arteriosclerosis of the brain
stem.
Left knee, gives out.
Cannot walk up stairs without aid.

10. Dance.

Off balance, the left knee failing, toppling.

11. Live.

CHARITY. Spine.
Spinal arthritis.
Now, after the years, he is humpbacked.
Vertebrae at the top of his back, collapsed, the bones
impacted, wedge-shaped bodies.

PALMER (*muttering*). So the vicious old bastard was old?
What do you want? Pity?

CHARITY *ignores that.*

CHARITY. Spinal deformity thrusts the head forward.
Limits traverse movement, side to side, no more than
a few degrees left, a few degrees right.
Cannot raise his head.
When he tries, he becomes dizzy and can fall.

12. Dance.

The spine, the fear of falling.

13. Live.

Following the tape.

CHARITY. Cannot wash the back of his neck.
Has to shave, sitting, with an electric razor.
And so he walks.
Shuffling.
Bent forward at a sharp angle.
Holding the arm of a guard.
To the prison garden.
At half past two in the afternoon, of the 17th of
August, 1987.

14. Tape.

*A montage, using and developed from the photograph of Rudolph
Hess walking in the garden of Spandau. Black and white charcoal
drawings follow the narrative, mixing with and developing from
close-ups of* CHARITY *miming the hanging with the length of flex.*

15. Live.

CHARITY *takes a piece of flex, exactly the same as that on
the tape, from the video trolley.*

*In her mime she distorts herself into the careful, frail
movements of a very old, decrepit body.*

CHARITY. The garden.
Trees, overgrown.
One prisoner, in the huge building. Year on year.
Guards changed, four nations, each month.
The Soviets in July.
The Americans in August.

In September, the British.

Endless routine.

Old concrete, set.

And in the routine, neglect. In the cracks of the years, little carelessnesses.

The trees in the garden have grown, higher than the watchtowers.

Quarter past three in the afternoon.

The guard in Tower B sees Hess and his duty warder, sitting together, on a bench.

The duty warder is called back to the main cell block, a telephone call, the subject of the call – never disclosed.

Because of the trees the guard in Tower B cannot see the summerhouse.

The summerhouse, a wooden, rectangular hut, used by the gardener to store his tools.

A beam, six foot from the ground.

A work bench.

A sharpening wheel.

Two pairs of shears.

Rags on the bench.

Old garden chairs.

A garden hose, coiled.

On the floor woodshavings, metal filings.

And two coils of yellow electric flex.

The warder returned.

Hess, crumpled against the garden chairs.

Half-sat, half-lain, bent forward, knees drawn to the chest, round his neck a length of flex, face dark blue.

They came running.

Pulled Hess out of the summerhouse.

Tried to revive. Resuscitation.

Smashed six of his ribs.

Stumbled and shouted.

Routine ended.

She has followed the mime through to its conclusion, ending as Hess dead.

16. Tape.

The tape ends. The screens snow.

III.

> CHARITY *stands. Then she dances the steps she has improvised together, ending with a dance presentation of Hess's end. The impossibility of him hanging himself. A death by being strangled from behind. Graceful, beautiful, in silence but for the squeak of her shoes upon the floor. She stops it, and is out of breath, collapsed, her head down. She looks up. She shrugs. She takes the flex from her neck and throws it to* PALMER, *who catches it.*

IV.

PALMER, *the length of flex in his hand. He looks at it.*

> *A silence.*

CHARITY. The yellow electric flex. Left by employees of the firm Frohberg Elektrobau. They had been working in Spandau that day. Repairing the 4,000 volt wire, around the gaol's perimeter.

PALMER. But the statement by the four powers said – wait. *Flicks with his remote control. Rewinds. Plays.*

TAPE. . . . Hanged himself from a window latch in a small summerhouse in the prison garden, using an electrical extension cord which had for some time been kept in the summerhouse for use in connection with a reading lamp. Attempts . . .

> *He stops the tape.*

CHARITY. The reading lamp had been removed many years before, when the prisoner's eyes had weakened and he could no longer read.

PALMER. But so trivial a detail.

CHARITY. Yes.

PALMER. Why is it wrong in the official statement?

> *A silence.*

CHARITY. The report also did not say that the flex had been wiped with a rag. The rag was soaked in Acetone. Acetone is a fat and oil solvent, which gives off a smell of nail varnish.

PALMER. Was there mention of Acetone being kept in the summerhouse?

CHARITY. No.

PALMER. Acetone, could its smell, its fumes, knock you out? Like chloroform?

CHARITY. No.

A silence.

PALMER. Why was the flex wiped, anyway?

CHARITY. I am sure you know the answer to that. Don't you read detective novels?

He pauses.

PALMER. You want me to say the flex was wiped clean by Hess's murderer, before strangling him. The murderer would, of course, have worn leather gloves. As all the murderers do.

CHARITY. As all the murderers do.

She pauses.

When a man hangs the body's fall drags the knot, up to the highest point of the loop.

PALMER. Ah.

He pauses.

Ah.

CHARITY. As the knot pulls away from the back of the neck, it leaves no mark. But the marks on the throat will be of equal intensity, all along the throat. But the autopsy on Hess's body showed the mark was not equal on the throat. It was slanting, thickest over the adam's apple, by a twist, by a knot, by a knot twisted, by a hand.

PALMER. A hand in a leather glove.

He smiles and sighs. Suddenly she snatches the flex from his hand. She whirls away, a fury of movement.

CHARITY. Old man, hang himself? Tie a flex to a beam, a latch of a window? Tie the flex to his neck?

She mimes the elderly Hess trying to do so. 'He' cannot. He stumbles and falls to the floor, his body stiff, the flex in a shaking hand. Then she relaxes, her body loose.

PALMER. This material was collected by your husband.

CHARITY. Yes.

PALMER. Your memory is very good.

CHARITY. He was one of them.

PALMER. I'm sorry?

CHARITY. My husband was one of the specialists.

A pause.

One of the committee of specialists.

PALMER. There was a committee, of which Istvan Luber was a member? A committee, to do with the death of Rudolf Hess?

CHARITY. You didn't know?

PALMER *looks down.*

You are making me nervous, Mr Palmer. You have a reputation of being an investigative journalist, 'in the know'. A rather fearsome reputation. But you have never heard of the United States and United Kingdom Emergency Co-ordinating Committee?

PALMER. Forgive me, I feel a lemon.

CHARITY. The USUKEMCOC?

PALMER. Specialists? What, to advise . . . ? An ad hoc committee, set up by the British and the Americans?

CHARITY. I did trust you to know. That's why I agreed to see you, only you, and not any of the other freaks . . .

PALMER. I won't disappoint you, Frau Luber. I am a fast learner.

CHARITY. Are you?

They look at each other. A pause.

PALMER. Had this committee met before?

CHARITY. Oh yes, at crucial times.

PALMER. Such as?

CHARITY *shrugs.*

The Soviets weren't involved?

CHARITY. No, of course not.

PALMER. The French?

CHARITY. There was a French woman there.

PALMER. And the committee's purpose was to . . . what?

She shakes her head, looking down. PALMER, *irritated.*

You'll have to tell me more, Frau Luber. I don't want
to be rude, but last week I met a man who believes
there are two moons circling the earth. What was the
brief of this committee?

CHARITY. To tell lies.

PALMER. Disinformation?

CHARITY. Lies.

She still looks down.

PALMER. Who were the other members of the committee,
beside your husband?

She stands. She shakes her head.

I would like to contact them. I need corroboration . . .

CHARITY. They're dead. Like Istvan.

PALMER. I see.

A silence.

CHARITY. They went into the walls.

PALMER *takes a deep breath and blows air out. He runs his
hand through his hair.*

PALMER. There is a ship. *The Reefer Rio*, registered in
   Panama. It is carrying 6,000 tonnes of radioactive beef,
   from EEC surplus stores. The beef is from Ireland and
   Denmark, it was contaminated by fallout from the
   Chernobyl accident. The beef arrived in Venezuela.
   The authorities refused to let it into the country,
   because of excessive levels of radioactive caesium.
   Since then the ship has been sailing around the world
   for a year, looking for a buyer. It is a good story. I
   sold it to Reuters.

   CHARITY *walks away.*

CHARITY. Where is the ship now?

PALMER. It was last reported to be sailing to Poland.

   CHARITY *nods, looking down.*

   Meanwhile, Rudolf Hess was murdered? As the
   radioactive meat set out upon its journey around the
   earth? Is that what you are telling me?

CHARITY. I don't see the connection.

PALMER. There is none. None at all. Except for the
   insanely paranoid. And the odd poet amongst us.

   *She throws the flex on the floor. She turns on him in a fury,
   fists clenched. A moment, both still, then she turns and goes.*

V.

PALMER *stands and goes to the video trolley. He leans against it,
looking down. Then he realises it is piled with video tapes, in
disorder. He picks up one. It has no markings. He shrugs. He puts it
into the player and starts it. The audience see the same tape as he on
their machines.*

1. The Tape.

*A palimpsest of old TV shows, old movies, TV adverts, each very
quick. As if it is an old video tape that has been used again and*

again for recording television programmes. Electronic detritus: recorded by an obsessive TV watcher, perhaps a child.

2. *The tape snows, as if going to a different speed of recording.*

3. *Then a legend in black and white. The UN sign. Beneath it –*

UNESCO INTERNATIONAL STANDING COMMITTEE OF CULTURAL CO-ORDINATION (UNISICOC)

And at the bottom of the screen –

USUK EMCOC/cover 43/sub.P7/4887sectap003

4. *In black and white. The room represented by the tapestries. But the room on the video is 'real' – solid walls, panelling, a shiny floor. There is a set of grand double doors. In one of the walls, concealed by* trompe l'oeil *decoration, there is a small hidden door, the entrance to secret passages, which becomes apparent later. There are three gold chairs in the room. The shots on the video are made by four cameras, from ceiling height. They are obviously hidden security cameras. Each can pan in a narrow range. When they do so their movement is even, as if automatic. Each has two sets of focus, a wide shot, a narrow shot. The recording moves from one camera to another, but without the sense of 'making a good shot' – as if they are activated by where the voices in the room are coming from. The sound quality is 'dry' and loud.*

The room empty. The cameras rotate their shots evenly.

The double doors open. NICOLE *and a US Army* OFFICER *come into the room.* NICOLE *is thirty-three. She is dressed in a fine, conservative woman's suit. The* OFFICER's *uniform is immaculate.* NICOLE, *who is French, speaks English immaculately. She is pedantic. Her voice is deep.*

OFFICER.

This is the facility.

NICOLE.

Yes.

A silence.

OFFICER.

There will be a briefing at 19.00 hours. Thank you, Professor D'Arcy.

The OFFICER *turns to go.*

NICOLE.

Can I ask . . .

The OFFICER *stops.*

NICOLE.

Why I am here?

OFFICER.

That would be inappropriate at this time. I hope your room is satisfactory?

NICOLE.

The room looked excellent. The ceiling a mile high? With cupids and nudes, swimming in the clouds above? But the view through the window, a brick wall?

OFFICER.

We had to allocate rooms to members of the committee at pace. Perhaps later, we can relocate you.

NICOLE.

Can I ask where I am?

OFFICER.

This facility is made available courtesy of the Government of the Netherlands.

NICOLE.

So I am in Holland.

OFFICER.

Ah . . . Forgive me Professor D'Arcy.

NICOLE.

Inappropriate? At this time?

OFFICER.

The location of this facility is classified.

NICOLE.

I did see out of the helicopter? The military helicopter? That whirled me here from Paris? I do have eyes. I saw a lake? A lawn? Stone statues? A palace?

OFFICER.

Again, I have to ask you to forgive me, Professor. There is a strictly need-to-know continuity being maintained at this time.

NICOLE.

Lieutenant. The meetings of the UNESCO International Standing Committee of Cultural Co-ordination are not, usually, so . . . glamorous? UNISICOC is one of the most boring organisations I know. One does not usually step out of US Army helicopters into palaces to attend its deliberations.

OFFICER.

This is an emergency meeting, Professor.

NICOLE.

Can one have a cultural emergency? Has a symphony orchestra machine-gunned an audience?

OFFICER.

I have duties to attend to. This facility is being made operational at very short notice. Please forgive any inconvenience. The briefing will be at 19.00 hours.

Both still. Then the OFFICER *turns and goes, closing the double doors.* NICOLE *alone in the room. Irritable movements. She turns. She looks up at a camera.*

NICOLE.

Hello?

Her eyes drift from the camera. She has not seen it. But she has sensed the bugging. She goes to the centre of the room. Again she turns, then is still. The cameras return to the rhythm of shots they made when the room was empty.

The watching **LARRY PALMER** *shakes his head and leans forward, tired.*

5. *The rhythm of the cameras . . . One catches a small door open in the wall, behind* **NICOLE'***s back. It closes.*

> **LARRY PALMER** *has not seen it.*

6. *The rhythm of the cameras . . . Another catches another door, open, out of* **NICOLE'***s eyeline. The cameras switch.*

Again, **LARRY PALMER** *has not seen it. He looks at the screen again.*

7. *The rhythm of the cameras around* **NICOLE,** *all four cover the room. There is nothing untoward. Then a camera catches a hidden door open and a figure, just glimpsed, in late 17th century costume, a man, falling back into the dark beyond. The door closes. No sound.*

> **LARRY PALMER** *starts.*

LARRY *(under his breath . . .).* What the f. . .

8. *The double doors open.* **RAYMOND TRACE** *walks into the room. He is in his mid-forties, casually and rather shambolically dressed.* **NICOLE** *turns to him. They stare at each other. The cameras change their rhythm, picking up the sound.*

RAYMOND.

Hello Nicole.

A silence.

NICOLE.

Hello Raymond.

PALMER *stops the video machine. He plays the tape back and forth, searching. He finds the image of the hidden door open. He pauses the machine. The image is blurred and strange, the figure* *smeared. He rewinds a few frames. He plays it again. This time the figure is even more distinct. It plays on to* **RAYMOND***'s entrance.*

9. *On the tape –*

RAYMOND.

Hello Nicole.

PALMER *stops the tape. The frame frozen. He scrutinises the image. He rewinds, stopping every few frames. He reaches the sequence of the hidden door opening. He – and the audience on their monitors – are confronted by the figure. It is, for the third time, different. The resolution is still smeared but eerily, there are pale streaks of colouring about the clothing. The face is contorted.* **PALMER** *lights a cigarette. He plays the tape.*

10. . . . *The figure falls back into the dark beyond the door. The door closes. The double doors open.* **RAYMOND TRACE** *enters.* **NICOLE** *turns to him. They stare at each other. The cameras change their rhythm, picking up the sound.*

RAYMOND.

Hello Nicole.

A silence.

NICOLE.

Hello Raymond.

A silence. Then the tape snows, changing speeds. And there is more of the palimpsest of old TV programmes and adverts.

PALMER *goes to the machine. Fast forwards. The mush of old programmes continues. He stops the tape for a few seconds, continues to fast forward. He can find no more of the room. Eventually the tape snows into a unused section. He turns it off. He sits, smoking.*

PALMER. Into the walls.

VI.

Live performance. NICOLE *and the* OFFICER *come on.*

OFFICER. This is the facility.

NICOLE. Yes. (*Aside.*) Helicoptered
                            in, I fell
                                      to dreaming.

OFFICER. There will be a briefing at 19.00 hours. Thank
    you, Professor D'Arcy.

    The OFFICER *turns to go.*

NICOLE (*aside*). For fame
                            is like
                                    love

                    Fame flatters
                            fame smiles
                                    fame caresses

                    And makes your skin
                            feel just
                                    wonderful.

(*To the* OFFICER.) Can I ask . . .

    The OFFICER *stops.*

    Why I am here?

OFFICER. That would be inappropriate at this time. I
    hope your room is satisfactory?

NICOLE. The room looked excellent, the ceiling a mile
    high? With cupids and nudes, swimming in the clouds
    above? But the view through the window, a brick wall?

OFFICER. We had to allocate rooms to members of the
    committee at pace. Perhaps later, we can relocate you?

NICOLE. Can I ask where I am?

OFFICER. This facility is made available courtesy of the
    Government of the Netherlands.

NICOLE. So I am in Holland.

OFFICER. Ah . . . Forgive me Professor D'Arcy.

NICOLE. Inappropriate? At this time?

OFFICER. The location of this facility is classified.

NICOLE. I did see out of the helicopter? The military
    helicopter? That whirled me here from Paris? I do
    have eyes. I saw a lake? A lawn? Stone statues? A
    Palace?

(*Aside*.) This is fame's
                    pornography
                            the smooth

            Secrecy
                    the call
                            to the centre

            Of power
                    the libertine's
                            château

            The silent pilot
                    of the roaring
                            machine

            trying not to look
                    at my legs as I pull
                            the seat belt tight

            I
                    am
                            seduced

            Aie, aie Nicole
                    have you come
                            to this?

OFFICER. Again, I have to ask you to forgive me,
    Professor. There is a strictly need-to-know continuity
    being maintained at this time.

NICOLE (*aside*). All the young dudes
                    in uniform
                            he really

            Doesn't want to sweat
                    his collar up, he wants

                              his collar really clean . . .

(*To the* OFFICER.) Lieutenant. The meetings of the
    UNESCO International Standing Committee . . .

    (*Aside*.) Blah blah I go
                        No need to listen
                            to myself

                Always be
                        difficult on
                            arrival

                At airports
                        international
                            hotels

                Prickle and
                        be prickly
                            let them know

                You know
                        your
                            worth.

OFFICER. This is an emergency meeting, Professor.

NICOLE. Can one have a cultural emergency? Has a
    symphony audience machine-gunned an audience?

    The OFFICER *'mute', i.e. miming his next line, as* NICOLE
    speaks.

OFFICER (*mute*). I have duties to attend to. This facility is
    being made operational at very short notice. Please
    forgive any inconvenience. The briefing will be at
    19.00 hours.

NICOLE (*aside*). Though this
                    feels

                            strange

                No dust
                        in the

                            air. Bugged

                Bugged,
                    I

                            feel

            The air
                    drawn tight
                            strained

        Silence
                listen-
                        ing, I

        Feel
                migraine.
                        I –

Both still. Then the **OFFICER** *turns and goes, closing the double doors.* NICOLE *alone in the room. Irritable movements. She turns. She looks up.*

    Hello?

    Nothing.

VII.

. . . And **RAYMOND TRACE** *walks into the room. He stops dead still when he sees* **NICOLE.** *She turns. They look at each other.*

RAYMOND. Hello Nicole.

NICOLE. Hello Raymond.

    A silence.

RAYMOND. How was Los Angeles? I heard you were in Los Angeles.

NICOLE. In Los Angeles everyone is diseased. Love is coming to a stop.   AIDS

RAYMOND. So I hear. From promiscuity to celibacy in a generation?

NICOLE. A kind of purity is at work. The sexual plagues will free men and women.

RAYMOND. That pleases you?

NICOLE. It puts me very much at ease.

RAYMOND. Free of love? 'Cos no one will dare to sleep together anymore? If only that were true.

A pause. NICOLE *turning from him, in dislike.*

And how are post-semiological synthetics? Have I got that right?

NICOLE. You read my new book?

RAYMOND. Yes your book, great acclaim, great reviews. I must admit I read the reviews, not the work itself.

NICOLE. You are excused. After all we academics only write books to make each other feel bad, don't we?

RAYMOND. Becoming cynical, Nicole? Unlike you.

NICOLE. I . . .

RAYMOND. What?

A dismissive gesture from NICOLE.

NICOLE. And your work? How is vulgar Marxism?

RAYMOND. In the dog house. (*Aside.*) For I did love her once.

NICOLE (*aside*). Man, man, this man . . . Why do the unhappy have to be so repulsive? (*To* RAYMOND.) Why in the dog house?

RAYMOND. Comrade Gorbachev. The new line, glasnost and all that crap. Decades I and a few other comrades, kept the faith with the Soviet Union. Now the Soviets themselves turn round and tell us that the worker's paradise is a shit heap. All the arguments I spewed out for them, 'actually existing socialism' . . . Utterly discredited. The Politburo of the Soviet Union, voting for a free market? Coca Cola ads on Soviet TV? I feel betrayed.

NICOLE. No more Moscow freebies for you, then?

RAYMOND. I'm still big in Czechoslovakia.

A pause.

Well! Surprised to see you at this do.

NICOLE. Really, why?

RAYMOND. Bit down market for you, I'd have thought.

NICOLE. You know why we're here?

He stares at her.

RAYMOND. In het spoor van Willem en Mary.

She stares at him.

Glorieuze Revolutie. The Glorious Revolution of 1688.
I'm on the International Committee. Organised by the
Dutch Ministry of Foreign Affairs in co-operation with
the British Council. In samen werking met de Stichting
1688–1988.

NICOLE. Raymond, what are you talking about?

RAYMOND. William of Orange. Rent a King. 1688. They
needed a tame academic, to raise the tone, and I am
he.

NICOLE. Raymond . . .

RAYMOND. I know I know. Will'm 'n' Mary, just about
the most mind-fuckingly pointless bit of history
conceivable, but it pays well. Tricentennial
celebrations. International co-operation. It's one big
bloody wonderful freebie, actually. They put you up in
the American Hotel. They helicopter you to venues
like this. When does the meeting start then?

NICOLE. There has been some grotesque administrative
error.

RAYMOND. You're not here for the Will'm 'n' Mary
committee?

NICOLE. I'm here for UNISICOC.

RAYMOND. UNESCO Cultural Co-ordination. Bit out of
my league, old ducks. Oh to be on a UNESCO
committee. That is the flagship of freebies. UNESCO
is caviare and champagne, all round the world . . .
Well, what's your freebie about?

NICOLE. I was told it was an emergency.

RAYMOND. A cultural emergency? Did an audience machine gun a symphony orchestra?

NICOLE. Quite.

A silence.

The next UNISICOC meeting was going to be on Anti-Heideggerian strategies and feminist linguistics.

RAYMOND. Oh well. We'll do the two together. Heidegger meets William and Mary to discuss feminist linguistics. We are academics, we can bullshit our way out of that.

Shouting.

This is fucking typical of the fucking European Economic Community! Utterly fucking meaningless meetings! Everything to do with the European Economic Community is fucking meaningless! I will show you European Culture in a mountain of surplus butter!

NICOLE. This room is bugged.

A silence.

RAYMOND. How do you know?

NICOLE. Feel it.

A silence.

RAYMOND. I see what you mean.

He turns, calling.

Hey! Hey! When does the bar open?

CHARITY *comes on. She wears different clothes from before. Now she is in light blue jeans, a pink fluffy sweater and trainer shoes.*

CHARITY. Excuse me, can I ask you whether you smoke?

NICOLE *and* RAYMOND *look at her.*

If you do, can I ask you not to smoke? (*To* RAYMOND.) Excuse me Sir, but I notice you are wearing aftershave.

RAYMOND. Yes I am actually.

CHARITY. May I ask what brand?

RAYMOND. Kouros. You know, the advert on TV, with the racing driver . . .

CHARITY. It is not Old Spice?

RAYMOND. Bet your sweet life it is not. Look what . . .

CHARITY. Thank you for your help.

She turns away.

NICOLE. Oh God. Luber. (*To* CHARITY.) It's Istvan Luber, isn't it? (*To* RAYMOND.) He is allergic to tobacco smoke and Old Spice aftershave.

RAYMOND. Luber is here?

NICOLE. You are Professor Luber's assistant?

CHARITY (*to* NICOLE). I am his wife. (*To* RAYMOND.) My husband has provided historical material for this committee.

RAYMOND. Luber has provided material?

The OFFICER *enters. He carries folders, a clipboard, and video tapes.*

OFFICER. Professor D'Arcy, Professor Trace, thank you for your attention and for your presence here, under such pressure of time. (*To* CHARITY.) Is Professor Luber . . .

CHARITY. My husband is resting. He suggests the briefing begin. He will join you later.

RAYMOND. Oh will he.

OFFICER. The matter in hand for your consideration is of a highly classified nature. I cannot impress its seriousness upon you too greatly. Professor Trace, you have signed the Official Secrets Act.

A silence. CHARITY *slips away.*

RAYMOND. Have I?

OFFICER. For your work on the Home Office Anti-Terrorist Working Party.

RAYMOND. Fuck off soldier . . .

NICOLE. Raymond? You, the left-winger, have . . .

RAYMOND. That was in the early seventies, because of Ireland . . .

OFFICER. I have a photocopy here, of your declaration . . .

NICOLE. The rats of the left, gnaw each other?

She laughs.

RAYMOND. Shut up! You don't understand, I knew people.

NICOLE. What people?

RAYMOND. I knew people!

OFFICER (*to* NICOLE). Professor D'Arcy, the French Ministry of the Interior has vouchsafed for you. Your information leading to the arrest of Red Army Faction sympathizers in Lyons, in 1975 . . .

RAYMOND. Ah! Ah! But the lady wrote a famous defence of terrorism in 'Liberation'!

NICOLE. Cultural terrorism.

RAYMOND. Oh 'Cultural' terrorism. Pardonnez-moi.

NICOLE. It would seem, Raymond, we have both compromised for our countries: compromised and agonised. It would seem we are about to be asked to do so again.

RAYMOND (*to himself*). The dirt, the dirt, the dirt.

OFFICER (*to* NICOLE). The French Ministry of the Interior recommended you, Professor D'Arcy. The French Government is as concerned about the incident as are the Governments of the USA and of Britain.

RAYMOND. Incident?

OFFICER. The death of Rudolf Hess at 15.30 hours today.

A silence.

As expert media consultants and academics, the US and British authorities wish to have your recommendations as quickly as possible. Professor

Luber has prepared a briefing tape. Please give your attention to a console.

RAYMOND (*to* NICOLE). The death of Rudolf Hess. Tasty.

NICOLE (*to* RAYMOND). We are privileged. Perhaps.

OFFICER. This tape has been prepared by Professor Luber. Please attend.

RAYMOND *and* NICOLE *turn to screens. The* OFFICER *puts a tape in the machine – they use the same video trolley as* LARRY *used.*

The tape is speeding mishmash of Second World War German material.

The OFFICER *walks away from the trolley.*

VIII.

PALMER *goes to the trolley and stops the tape. He pauses.*

PALMER. The big
                story
                        the big

        Fish, out on the ocean
                a suitcase for a boat
                        wandering the world

        Sails the
                investigating
                        journalist

        I
                do
                        think.

He removes the tape. He scrabbles around amongst others. Some fall to the ground. He picks up one. He puts it on.

Tape: *On all the monitors – a palimpsest of TV 'channel hopping', in a montage with indistinct, cloudy video of love-making in a bed of many sheets. The man is never seen clearly,* *there is a glimpse of* CHARITY'*s face. It could be one of the home videos she referred to.*

PALMER *watches the screen for a while, then continues to speak.*

> Ernest Hemingway's
> > 'The Old Man
> > > And The Sea' –

He snorts.

> You lash
> > the fish
> > > to the boat

> And the sharks come
> > the denials
> > > contradictions

> Doubt
> > hearsay
> > > lies

> Gnaw away at the flesh
> > and when you reach the harbour
> > > what do you have? A

> Fishtail
> > a fishhead
> > > bones. 'The

> Great story' a wrecked kipper
> > on your hotel breakfast plate
> > > Ah well, you pay the bill

> Your gold card
> > takes the strain –
> > > the story's dead

> But one story
> > is just like
> > > another

> The planet
> > is crowded
> > > to death

> Everywhere

is becoming
like everywhere

Else, the same
beggars

Rangoon to London

The same money
Tokyo

to Delhi

The same TV
Beirut

to Berlin

I travel the world by Holiday Inn
the same room, same cabled porn
Cairo, Manila, Chicago, London

News

is news

is news

Anything
is anything
is anything

And truth?

He snorts.

Wearied away
in the weary seas

Of the weary
earth.

The tape snows.

Oh come
on, come on.

He walks away from the video trolley.

IX.

RAYMOND *goes to the video trolley and switches the tape off.*

From a projector on to a tapestry looms the photograph of Goering and Hess in the dock at Nuremberg. Goering is laughing at Hess from behind his hand.

NICOLE *has a microphone and is reading from notes, the 'recommendations' of the Committee.*

RAYMOND *is staring at the photograph as he eats a plateful of food with a fork.*

They are both exhausted.

NICOLE. Recommendation three. That the statement by the four powers be short. Five paragraphs, no more.

RAYMOND. The purity of the brief, official statement. *(Musing.)* At Nuremberg, why was Goering always laughing at Hess?

NICOLE *looks up.*

'Old comrades.' From the Munich Bierkeller putsch days in Munich. I mean, in the bickering at Hitler's court, Himmler was Hess's enemy, not Goering. Goering let Hess fly his aeroplanes.

He eats. (Mouth full.) This riz de veau truffés à la crême is excellent. Did they move a cook in for us?

He stands, holding up his plate. He speaks to the bugging.

Compliments to the chef.

He goes to the blown-up photograph.

NICOLE. Recommendation four. Security after the announcement of the death. Strict control by the military police of all of the prisoner's effects, and the prison fabric itself. It is essential that no bricks, window latches, piping, roof slating etcetera etcetera, no artifacts whatsoever from the prison are allowed to leave the site.

RAYMOND *(waving at her, still staring at the photograph).*

'Demolition of the myth . . .' Keep that paragraph.

NICOLE (*irritated*). Recommendation five. The site house where the prisoner died and all its contents must be burnt at once. Recommendation six. The demolition of Spandau Prison must begin at once. Military personnel should be used, not private contractors, to guard against any market in souvenirs. It is not a prison that is being demolished, it is an historical, or anti-historical, myth.

RAYMOND. What did Goering mean when he laughed in court, at Nuremberg, and said to Hess 'Are you going to tell us your big secret now?'

NICOLE. Recommendation six. When the prison has been demolished, it should not be left derelict, or, worse still, made into a public park. There must be no shrine. We suggest that the site be sold to a commercial enterprise for immediate development. To demythologise the ground upon which Spandau gaol once stood, a supermarket should be built there.

RAYMOND. We didn't discuss that!

NICOLE. Luber sent it down.

RAYMOND. From his sick bed above? (*He waves his fork at the ceiling.*) Nice one Istvan.

NICOLE. Recommendation seven. A strategy against demonstrations at the prison, on the announcement of the death. We suggest that, within two hours of the announcement, a small right-wing demonstration be staged at the prison gate by German security forces, posing as Neo-Fascist sympathizers. That television and press be advised of the demonstration in advance. The demonstration to be broken up by uniformed police, without incident. This will one – pre-empt any demonstration by the real right-wing, and two – satisfy the extreme left, that the right has been made to look ridiculous and give the left no reason to demonstrate themselves. There must be neither mourning on the right, nor celebration on the left. Recommendation eight, the Hess family. We suggest that, to counter an inflammatory statement by the Hess family, the

question of the burial be handled in this way. One –
an announcement will be made that the body will be
buried in the family plot. The world's press is to be
encouraged to descend upon the family. The body will
be given to the family on the understanding that it will
be buried elsewhere, secretly. Cremation would be
ideal, but this should not be sought, as the Hess
family is, nominally, Catholic. A further concession, to
be used in negotiation with the family, can be that the
body will be buried in the family plot, in nine months
time, but without publicity and at night. I am
exhausted.

She sits down.

RAYMOND. Are we done?

NICOLE. And I need a bath.

RAYMOND. Why did Hess claim amnesia when he went to
England? On his mad flight? This was a powerful
political head. But interrogation in England, nothing.
All his replies were imprecise. And why . . . in gaol,
did he refuse to meet his wife? For twenty-eight years
in Spandau, he never saw her.

NICOLE. The psychiatric report . . . 'An individual of a
superior intelligence with schizoid traits . . .' It was a
filthy mind. It went to pieces. We have buried the
pieces. I am exhausted and I need a long hot bath . . .

RAYMOND. There were six war criminals with him in
Spandau at first. The last to be released was Speer.
Speer said Hess never reminisced. While the good old
boys were going over tales of the good old days with
Adolf, Hess always slunk away. Walked in another part
of the prison garden. Kept himself apart.

*He goes right up to the photograph, running his hands over it.
The tapestry moves.*

We have buried the pieces. I feel kind of dirty, too.

NICOLE. Don't become sentimental. This is cultural
warfare. This is against fascism.

RAYMOND. It's gross media manipulation and we know it.

NICOLE. It is . . . an encoding of the truth. No more no
less. Our statement is a construct. Like any sentence,
or photograph.

RAYMOND. Or the Mona Lisa.

NICOLE. We construct it for the good.

RAYMOND. How Goebbels would have loved modern
literary theory.

He turns and calls out to the bugging.

We've done, boys! Come 'n' get it!

X.

The photograph disappears. Light change. The RAYMOND *and*
NICOLE *actors stay where they are, sitting on their chairs.*

LARRY PALMER *stands. He goes to the video trolley.* CHARITY
comes on. She is dressed as before in the scenes with PALMER.

PALMER *turns to her.*

PALMER. When did your husband die? While the
committee was in session?

CHARITY *says nothing. She goes to the video and extracts the
tape. She looks at it.*

CHARITY. You are a spy.

PALMER. Did you smuggle the tapes of the committee
out? Copy them illegally?

CHARITY. Everything leaks, somewhere, Mr Palmer.
People leak too. They leave trails in the minds of other
people.

He hesitates.

PALMER. When you said the members of the committee
died . . .

She stares at him.

When you said they went into the walls. What did you mean?

CHARITY, *upset, fumbles amongst video tapes. She finds the one she is looking for and puts it in the machine. She presses 'play'. On all the monitors, an amateur video of Cologne Cathedral appears. Colour, grainy quality. The hand-held camera pans around – the cathedral, towering into a grey sky.*

Cologne Cathedral?

CHARITY. Istvan took this.

The camera pans away to the shopping precinct before the cathedral, which is now out of sight.

Anywhere in Europe, no Mr Palmer? Any shopping mall. In England, in France.

He pauses.

Or where Spandau Prison stood?

The camera pans to the cathedral again.

The trouble with Cologne Cathedral is that it's not really there.

PALMER. Another quote from Istvan?

She stops the tape. She presses a rewind button.

What happened to your husband and that committee?

She stops the tape. She presses 'play'. She walks away, ignoring him. PALMER *is left alone staring at the screen. It snows. He wipes his eyes.*

XI.

The tape plays, **PALMER** *at the machine, leaning on his knuckles, crumpled before the screen.*

The Tape.

1. *In black and white a degraded shot of a military jet transport plane with FDR markings, taking off, into an overcast sky. It repeats itself, odd cutting.*

CHARITY (voice over).

Three hundred years from now, history students are shown a tape of a jet taking off. The students are told – this is Hitler, flying to meet Winston Churchill in 1941. But Hitler never met Churchill. And there were no jet planes in the Second World War. But there is the tape, three hundred years old.

A shot of Hitler from archive footage by a plane's window, looking out.

CHARITY (voice over).

There is the plane. There is Hitler. There is Hitler on the plane.

2. *A palimpsest of TV gameshows. Then it snows.*

> **PALMER** *stops the tape. He fast forwards it. He leans forward, shoulders rounded. He chants, like a child's rhyme.*

PALMER. See it now, you don't, now you see it, now . . .

He plays the tape.

3. *The room, again recorded by the four cameras.* **RAYMOND** *is turning to them, calling.*

RAYMOND.

We've done, boys! Come 'n' get it!

At once the double doors open. The **OFFICER** *pushes a trolley into the room. On the trolley there is an immaculate white tablecloth, dishes of food and two bottles of champagne in ice buckets.*

RAYMOND.

Hey hey, our masters have opened the bar.

He lifts a champagne bottle and starts work on the cork.

OFFICER.

We have to thank you for your work here at USUK-EMCOC.

RAYMOND.

You suck what?

OFFICER.

USUK Emergency Command Centre, of which your committee is an initiative.

RAYMOND.

You heard of this USUK?

NICOLE.

Acronyms are the codes of sin. I heard a rumour.

OFFICER.

A digest of your report has already been transmitted to Berlin. Your recommendations will form the basis of the Allied position in this matter.

NICOLE.

Has . . . this committee been active in the past?

RAYMOND.

There will be no answer to that. Will there, soldier?

Nothing from the **OFFICER.**

Who will write the history of the rewriters of history?

He pops the champagne cork.

OFFICER.

Cars to Schipol Airport are at your disposal. If you wish please continue to use the facility for another 24 hours. The kitchen will remain open for another 24 hours.

He turns to go.

RAYMOND.

He abandons us.

OFFICER.

You have contributed to the peace, Professor.

RAYMOND.

Knocked down Spandau Gaol and built a supermarket? Yeah. OK.

The OFFICER, *irritated for the first time.*

OFFICER.

Peace is a complex status to maintain.

NICOLE.

'A complex status.'

The OFFICER *salutes and goes.*

RAYMOND.

Ah well. Back to writing brochures for William 'n' Mary.

He swigs from the champagne bottle, wipes his mouth on his sleeve. NICOLE *looks directly at camera 1, up in the ceiling's corner.*

NICOLE.

To market history. On the shelves.

(To camera 2.)

NICOLE.

To remove impurities. To add artificial sweeteners.

(To camera 3.)

NICOLE.

So that tomato soup from the packets may be the colour of tomatoes. So that the news of the day may be black and white.

(*To camera 4.*)

NICOLE.

Why was cooking invented? As a measure against the near poison of everything we eat.

(*To camera 1.*)

NICOLE.

So cook the news. Reality is salmonella.

She looks at cameras 2, 3 and 4 in turn. The tape snows.

PALMER *switches the tape off and walks away, as . . .*

XII.

Live.

RAYMOND. We've done, boys! Come 'n' get it!

At once the double doors open. The **OFFICER** *pushes a trolley into the room. On the trolley an immaculate white tablecloth, dishes of food and two bottles of champagne in ice buckets.*

OFFICER (*aside*). General Patton
                    return to earth
                        zap these smucks.

RAYMOND. Hey hey, our masters have opened the bar.

OFFICER (*aside*). It's hard
                    to hear the bugles
                        forty and more

            Years on
                    Sicily
                        D Day

                    The Battle of the Bulge
                          just sound like old
                                junk movies on TV.

RAYMOND. You suck what?

OFFICER (*aside*). It's hard to hear the bugles calling
                          in the traffic on the autobahn
                                hard in a Hamburg bar.

RAYMOND (*to* NICOLE). You heard of this USUK?

NICOLE (*aside*). To market
                          history
                                remove

              Impurities
                    add harmless
                          sweeteners.

OFFICER (*aside*). War graves get forgot
                          Europe goes to the beach –
                                soldier boy on guard –

              Kids in the sand at the picnic
                    slop the mayonnaise
                          on the soldier's boots.

NICOLE (*aside*). Tomato soup
                          is the colour
                                of tomatoes

              The news
                    is on

                          the packet.

OFFICER.   And peace
                          is pissed
                                away.

RAYMOND (*to* NICOLE). He means yes.

NICOLE (*aside*). Reality
                    is sal –

                          monella.

OFFICER (*aside*). Where is the victory?

    He turns to go.

RAYMOND. You're abandoning us?

OFFICER (*aside*).   Peace is a complex
                                    status to maintain.

RAYMOND. Knocked down Spandau Prison and built a
     supermarket? Yeah. OK.

NICOLE. 'A complex status.'

The OFFICER *salutes and goes.*

XIII.

Live. RAYMOND *sipping champagne.* NICOLE *is making up,
with a hand mirror.* RAYMOND, *suddenly still.*

RAYMOND. Hey! The bugging's off.

NICOLE. What?

A silence.

RAYMOND. I miss it.

CHARITY *comes on, dressed for the committee, as before. She
has a video cassette in her hand.*

*Her hands are dirty. There are smudges of ash on her clothng
and her face.*

They stare at her.

NICOLE. What have you done?

CHARITY. Istvan.

RAYMOND. Your hands . . .

CHARITY. Nothing.

NICOLE. What's happened?

CHARITY *refuses to look at her.*

CHARITY. Istvan . . . has made this tape. He wants you to
     see it.

RAYMOND. What do you mean he's made a tape, he

wants us to see it? Treating us with contempt, sending edicts down through his sidekick. It's bloody outrageous.

NICOLE. Be quiet Raymond. (*To* CHARITY.) Has there been an accident? Is your husband alright?

CHARITY. He's sleeping now.

NICHOLE. You must tell us . . .

RAYMOND. Yeah, of course. Should we tell the goons here, to get a doctor in?

CHARITY. No.

A pause.

When my husband's slept, he will come down to see you. Now, see the tape he has made. Please.

She holds it out. RAYMOND *and* NICOLE *look at each other again.*

RAYMOND. If that is what the great man wants.

RAYMOND *takes the tape from* CHARITY. *He puts it into a machine and runs it.*

LUBER*'s video is made with a camcorder, handheld. He has, at times, tried to record himself in a mirror as he talks, but a camera light shines into the mirror. The screens 'white out', colours stream. Sometimes there is a glimpse of the video camera, but never of* LUBER*'s face.*

His breathing is bad. His voice is deep with a faint edge of a German accent.

LUBER.

My esteemed colleagues, you must forgive me I . . . Have wanted to join you, but the vagaries of health, one's tenuous grip on existence . . One wakes, one breathes, one has the illusion of safety . . . One second, one second, forgive me . . .

Violent coughing, the tape is stopped, then started again, the camera whirling.

RAYMOND. Jesus Christ, what's the matter with him?

LUBER.

. . . Satisfy your curiosity as to my condition . . . One pays for a holistic view of life, the holistic assault . . . the absurd project that one lives, that everything will mean everything else, thought, sleep, food, reading, language, love, that all will be imploded into one way of living . . . what you want Raymond, to be the renaissance man, but as your weltanschauung failed, your world view, the Marxist millenium, so has my stomach . . . It is the oyster in the shell that has done for me . . . where does the drive to human wholeness lead? Like Galileo, to grossness, obscenity, obsession . . .

A retching fit.

RAYMOND. What is he gibbering about? (*To* CHARITY.) What the hell is wrong with him?

LUBER.

I have for some years become inordinately fond of oysters . . . Not for me, the tangerine dreams of alcohol, Raymond, not for me the heady pursuit of power in excellence, Nicole . . . both addictions, corruscating, dissolving all judgement in the end, all self-respect . . .

Shouts.

Oh this fucking technology, how can one catch thought . . .

RAYMOND. (*To* NICOLE). He's having a go at you, now.

NICOLE. (*To* CHARITY). Is this all your husband . . .

CHARITY. Please pay attention.

The camera steadies. A tray on wheels, stacks of seafood plates piled high with oyster shells, bits of bread, squeezed pieces of lemon, a table napkin glimpsed, spotted with blood. Then the camera into the mirror.

LUBER.

. . . An intellectual passion to understand the world, can, what? Become a desire to eat the world? That is

my fate, my dear colleagues, to degenerate to gluttony.
With me it is oysters . . . Fragments of shells have
perforated my intestine . . . I was always a messy eater,
bolted my food, many do who come from where I
come from . . . I relish this absurdity, to die . . .

NICOLE. Die?

LUBER.

. . . in this way, cut to pieces by a luxury food, the
absurdity of someone like me who believes in the
unity of mind and body in this predicament . . .

A violent coughing fit.

LUBER.

Listen to me! Listen to me! My colleagues of
thoughtfulness, my comrade intellectuals, I have
information. Look! Look!

*The camera moves along the disordered bed. Documents are
spread out. Here and there, an oyster shell.*

LUBER.

I have withheld these documents from you . . . Vanity,
vanity, I was going to crack the truth of this hard shell,
this pearl in the slime . . .

RAYMOND *(overlapping)*. For fucksake, Luber imagery . . .

LUBER.

. . . black pearl of disgust, the truth of this vile matter
. . . Rudolf Hess, his war record, 1914 to 1918 . . . 8th
August, 1917 . . . Severely wounded in the left lung by
a rifle bullet . . . The bullet penetrated the chest, right
through the chest. Right through the body . . . Hess
was in various war hospitals until 10th of December,
1917.

The camera zig-zags away from the bed.

RAYMOND. So? The bastard was a war hero.

The camera is now zooming to the X-ray of a man's chest.

The X-ray is pinned up against a photographer's lamp.

NICOLE. Hess?

CHARITY. Yes.

LUBER.

This X-ray was taken in the British Military Hospital in Berlin, September 1973.

RAYMOND. X-Ray. Common image of humanity. Could be you, me, Hitler, Hess, Tutankhamen, Jesus Christ.

NICOLE (*sotto*). No bullet wound.

LUBER.

See it, see it, do we see it, history, the trace, the mark left by the truth of a great lie? Look! . . .

No sign of damage to the ribs on the left side.

No dead tissue track through the lung, which a rifle bullet must leave.

A silence.

On the tape, the X-ray is beginning to smoke with the heat from the light.

At the X-Ray session, the doctor asked – 'Was ist passiert mit den Kriegsunfallen? Nicht hauttief?'

NICOLE. 'What happened to your war wounds? Not even skin deep?'

A silence. The X-ray smoking.

RAYMOND. The X-ray, he's letting it . . .

LUBER.

The prisoner replied 'zu spät, zu spät!'

NICOLE. 'Too late, too late.'

LUBER.

And his bowels opened.

He messed the floor.

They led him away to the bathroom.

At Spandau Prison, on July 7th 1987, there was an emergency . . . The prisoner was raving. He wanted to confess. After all the years, confess what? What?

RAYMOND. The fucking thing is burning!

And on the tape the camera held anyhow, a hand pulling at the X-ray, now alight . . .

LUBER.

Oh! Oh!

And the tape cuts to a little later. The X-ray, ruined, a hole melted in its centre, lies on the bed, smeared with ash.

LUBER.

Hess not Hess.

The man who died in Spandau, was not Hess.

LUBER, *now speaking in great pain.*

What is history? The real Hess took off, over the North Sea. To be shot down on Himmler's orders. Raymond, what you know of the Nazi Party, think! A medieval court. Conspirary within conspiracy. One of Himmler's agents flew a second plane, out to discredit Hitler. With a message, that Hitler be replaced, along with Churchill.

What is it: This thing, this state of mind . . . History? That we bend, that we distort? From which we want . . . *The truth?*

RAYMOND (*overlapping*). What's the bastard doing? Destroying evidence, wrecking our work, what?

LUBER.

Raymond, Nichole, do you understand what we have done? . . . Ours in the new treason of the clerks . . . We have become specialists, technicians of acceptable truths . . . this is a new age, that only has use for our expertise . . . it has seduced us . . . We are morticians, we deliver history with an acceptable face . . . acceptable facts, which may or may not be true . . .

but they are safe . . . to be taught on the Modern
History exam syllabus . . .

The camera turns to the mirror.

LUBER.

And it is too late, for us to extricate ourselves, zu spat,
zu spat . . .

The camera turns to the bed, LUBER's *hand striking matches,
the war records begin to burn.*

Then as if LUBER *falls with the camera to the floor. The
camera is pointing at the door of the room.* CHARITY *is
coming into the room.*

And, abruptly, the tape stops.

RAYMOND. Hess not Hess.

NICOLE. Hess was in prison. He died there. That was
what Hess was for. Prisoner number 7. He died in
Spandau. It was on the news tonight.

RAYMOND. The news we made, for fucksake!

NICOLE. Yes. (*To* CHARITY.) Is . . .

CHARITY *turns away.* RAYMOND *strides to the doors. He
cannot open them.*

You out there! What has happened to our colleague?
You!

A silence.

We . . . withdraw our report! Can you hear? You out
there!

NICOLE. The report will stand. It's on the news, now. And
it is inconceivable. The years, years and years, twisted.
In twisted loyalty, alone in Spandau. A false Hess?
How could he have stood it?

RAYMOND. Maybe he was waiting for orders.

A silence.

We must . . .

NICOLE. What? Denounce our own work? What official evidence, what single mark will there be . . . that we ever met? We have been traduced.

She starts. CHARITY *moves to a corner.*

The cameras? . . .

CHARITY *puts a finger to her lips.*

RAYMOND (*low*). Bastards. Bastards. Bastards.

NICOLE. Rudolf Hess killed himself in Spandau Prison on the 17th of August, 1987.

RAYMOND. Yeah. It was on the news, no?

CHARITY *gestures to them.*

CHARITY. Come, now!

CHARITY *crouches by a wall and pushes open a small concealed door.* NICOLE *and* RAYMOND *approach it carefully.*

NICHOLE. The smell . . . of the air in there.

NICOLE *and* RAYMOND *go through the little door.*

RAYMOND (*from within*). What's that, hanging there?

CHARITY *closes the door.*

XIV

PALMER *turns and sees* CHARITY. *He stares at her.*

PALMER. This what they let you do in here? You have the expertise. Didn't you work as a TV producer for RTF?

CHARITY. You have done your research, Mr Palmer.

PALMER. Oh I do my research. You left French TV, some kind of breakdown even then wasn't it? You dropped out, became a student in Geneva, shacked up with the great Professor Luber?

A silence.

What, the doctors let you fake up tapes? Part of the swish psychotherapy is it, in between sipping the spa waters and being hosed down? To fake up history?

CHARITY. You are cruel.

PALMER *sighs.*

PALMER. Yeah, sorry about that. (*Putting his tape-recorder into his briefcase.*)

CHARITY. Aren't you going to talk to them?

A silence.

PALMER. Talk to who?

CHARITY. The walls.

He stares at her.

The walls beyond the walls, in the room. That you can get to, through a little door.

But you'll get into the paintings, on the walls.

Haven't you seen them?

PALMER. I . . .

CHARITY. Huge ugly things, the paint going dark, even the new painting, heavy and thick. The paint . . . hanging there, in folds.

We're there, we've been painted in.

PALMER. Look . . .

CHARITY. Istvan. You. Me.

PALMER. What . . . What happened to the other two? Raymond, Nicole? Painted on these walls, you're talking about?

CHARITY. They died, in a plane crash. On an internal flight, Moscow to Riga, in the Soviet Union.

She huddles against the wall.

PALMER. Yeah. Those internal flights in the Soviet Union. I sat by a door, of some Illyushin crate, water was pouring in, right through the flight.

A pause.

So they got together, did they? Across the ideological divide? They seemed to loathe each other.

Nothing from CHARITY.

If that really was them, eh? On your tape.

(*He walks away from her.*)

XV.

CHARITY (*aside*). Constanza.

A pause.

> Constanza
> > when Mozart died

> Held his body in her arms
> > for four hours
> > > then they had

> To drag her screaming
> > from the bed –
> > > Simone.

Pause.

> Simone de Beauvoir
> > when Jean Paul Sartre died
> > > wanted to do the same

> A nurse said 'no
> > don't do that
> > > the gangrene –'

Pause.

> I made a promise
> > when you died
> > > to say just once

> All the things
> > you said to me –
> > > in memory

Once to someone
    no matter who
        a stranger

In the street
    to a cold
        tape machine

A scribble
    on a misted
        windowpane

In eternal memory
    however fleeting, and when I've done
        go south, and be young

Again.
    But.

A pause.

    But
        I begin

To forget –
    what did you say?
        I reinvent –

Constanza
    Simone
        my love

Rots in my arms
    his memory
        glues my skin

Constanza
    Simone
        help me

I am condemned
    to the holy fury
        of Antigone.

XVI.

CHARITY *crouched by the wall.* PALMER, *aside.*

PALMER. I didn't write up the 'Was Hess Hess?' story. A
mate of mine on *The Guardian* was deep into all that
anyway, risking his sanity.

A pause.

So, I just left her there. That was the autumn of '88.
The spring of '89, I learnt she'd left that place where
I'd interviewed her, the millionaires' funny farm in the
Austrian Alps. There was a full colour pic. of her in
Vogue magazine. She'd married an American
businessman. Big, I read, in the world of Transatlantic
trusts.

A pause.

In the *Vogue* pic, she looked a million dollars, she was
leaning against this guy, the new husband. He had a
face like a wall. Deep eyes, of pale aquamarine, going
on to blue. A handsome bastard, almost beautiful.
And she, ah she . . . was wearing a cream silk trouser
suit, NVPL – no visible panty line. I got nowhere near
what that woman was about, I thought, nowhere near.
I felt . . . abused. And I'd had the nerve to fancy her.

He shakes his head.

Ships in the night.

A pause.

And now all this. In the last few weeks, the latest High
Society New York murder case. That woman, who
slammed a hypodermic into her husband's chest while
he slept? A massive dose of adrenalin, straight into the
heart? That is her.

I've done a piece on it for the *New York Post*, a big
break for me. 'I met murderess in Nazi loony bin'
'cetera, 'cetera.

The thing is though, the second husband, face like a
wall, flat like a wall, deep, pale blue eyes, handsome,

almost beautiful. He was half the age, but very like
Rudolf Hess.

He leaves.

XVII.

CHARITY, *still crouched, lifts a remote control unit and presses the*
button.

Tape.

On the screens the legend:

> *THE WALLS OF SPANDAU SPEAK.*

The text is spoken by LUBER's *voice.*

The tape shows photographs, some official, some amateur, some black
and white, some coloured, of the demolition of Spandau Prison.

VOICE.   The day the Nazi died
                            his prison walls were just
                                   hard dust

             Waiting to be smashed
                      by demolition balls
                              swung from cranes to crack

             The hardened crust of that dead
                      history – the walls of Spandau
                              thought 'Why must

             They pulverise the memory
                      of the horror that we held
                              into thin air? We are free

             But the past falls with us –
                      we are dispelled
                              the old lies

             Are forgotten, we are
                      condemned, expelled
                              An unseen cloud

Of molecules blown
>over European skies
>>into the lungs

Of a bureaucrat on the 'phone
>Brussels to Paris, into
>>the innocent eyes

Of a child in a London park
>on to the feet
>>of irritating flies

Buzzing a Cannes icecream
>on to the dark lips
>>of a whore in Amsterdam

Into a German's beer –
>we are the dirty mark
>>the rain leaves on a Stockholm

Windowpane. We
>do not disappear
>>we were imprinted

By a monstrous pain
>we faced with stone
>>what you pretend

Was never there
>so! Check the food
>>the water and the air

We are in you
>and will rise again
>>we are cancer, we are there

We will be
>revenged
>>and rise again.'

The screens go dead. In the room, the audience and playing area, a blackout. The tapestries become see-through as lights rise upon wall paintings of the horrors of history, the actors caught, frozen, in the designs.

This play

is so

fooky cool!